Copyright © 2023 by Herman Strange (Author)

All rights reserved. This book or any portion thereof may not be reproduced or used in any manner whatsoever without the express written permission of the publisher except for the use of brief quotations in a book review.

This book is copyright protected. This is only for personal use. You cannot amend, distributor, sell, use, quote or paraphrase any part or the content within this book without the consent of the author. Please note the information contained within this document is for educational and entertainment purposes only. Every attempt has been made to provide accurate, up to date and reliable complete information. No warranties of any kind are expressed or implied.

Readers acknowledge that the author is not engaging in the rendering of legal, financial, medical or professional advice. The content of this book has been derived from various sources. Please consult a licensed professional before attempting any techniques outlined in this book.

By reading this document, the readers agree that under no circumstances are the author responsible for any losses, direct or indirect, which are incurred as a result of the use of information contained within this document, including but not limited to errors, omissions or inaccuracies.

Thank you very much for reading this book.

Title: Beyond the Hype-The Truth about Cryptocurrencies' Downsides and Dangers

Author: Herman Strange

Table of Contents

Introduction 6
    Definition of cryptocurrency 6
    Brief history of cryptocurrencies 8
    Importance of discussing the downsides of cryptocurrencies 10
    Overview of the six bad things to be discussed in the book 13

Chapter 1: Volatility 15
    Explanation of volatility in the cryptocurrency market 15
    Examples of extreme price fluctuations 18
    Factors that contribute to volatility 21
    Risks and Challenges for Investors 23

Chapter 2: Lack of Regulation 25
    Explanation of the lack of regulation in the cryptocurrency market 25
    Examples of fraudulent and illegal activities involving cryptocurrencies 27
    Potential risks for investors and the market as a whole 30
    Current State of Regulation and Future Prospects 32

Chapter 3: Security Risks 35

Explanation of the security risks associated with cryptocurrencies 35
Types of cyberattacks targeting cryptocurrency exchanges and wallets 37
Best practices for securing cryptocurrencies 40
Future developments in cryptocurrency security 44

Chapter 4: Environmental Impact 48
Explanation of the environmental impact of cryptocurrency mining 48
Comparison of energy consumption of cryptocurrency mining to traditional financial systems 52
The carbon footprint of cryptocurrency mining. 55
Potential solutions to reduce the environmental impact 58

Chapter 5: Lack of Acceptance 61
Explanation of the limited acceptance of cryptocurrencies in mainstream society 61
Reasons why businesses are hesitant to accept cryptocurrencies 65
Efforts to increase acceptance and adoption 67
Future outlook for cryptocurrency as a practical currency 70

Chapter 6: Complex Technology 72
    Explanation of the complex technology behind
    cryptocurrencies 72
    Barriers to adoption for the average person 75
    Opportunities and challenges for the future of
    cryptocurrency technology 77
    Potential for simplification and mass adoption . 80

Summary and Conclusion 82
    Recap of the six bad things associated with
    cryptocurrencies 82
    Reflection on the overall impact of
    cryptocurrencies on society 85
    Call to action for investors, businesses, and
    policymakers 87
    Final thoughts on the future of cryptocurrencies
    89

Potential References 91

Introduction

Definition of cryptocurrency

A cryptocurrency is a digital asset that is designed to work as a medium of exchange, using strong cryptography to secure financial transactions and control the creation of additional units. Cryptocurrencies operate independently of a central bank and are based on a decentralized, peer-to-peer network that uses blockchain technology to maintain a digital ledger of all transactions.

The first cryptocurrency, Bitcoin, was introduced in 2009 by an unknown person or group of people under the name Satoshi Nakamoto. Since then, the cryptocurrency market has grown rapidly, with thousands of different cryptocurrencies now available. Some of the most popular cryptocurrencies include Bitcoin, Ethereum, Ripple, and Litecoin.

The key feature that sets cryptocurrencies apart from traditional currencies is the use of cryptography to secure transactions and control the creation of new units. Cryptocurrencies use a system of public and private keys to secure transactions and ensure that only the owner of a particular cryptocurrency can make transactions with it. This makes cryptocurrencies much more secure than traditional currencies, which can be vulnerable to counterfeiting and other forms of fraud.

Another important feature of cryptocurrencies is their decentralized nature. Unlike traditional currencies, which are controlled by central banks, cryptocurrencies operate on a peer-to-peer network that is not controlled by any single entity. This makes them more resistant to government intervention and other forms of interference.

In addition to their use as a medium of exchange, cryptocurrencies can also be used for a variety of other purposes, such as digital identity verification, smart contracts, and secure storage of valuable assets.

While cryptocurrencies have the potential to revolutionize the way we think about money and financial systems, they are not without their drawbacks. In the following chapters of this book, we will explore some of the risks and challenges associated with cryptocurrencies, including their volatility, lack of regulation, security risks, environmental impact, lack of acceptance, and complex technology.

Brief history of cryptocurrencies

The idea of digital cash has been around since the early days of the internet, but it wasn't until 2009 that the first cryptocurrency, Bitcoin, was created by an unknown person or group of people using the pseudonym Satoshi Nakamoto. Bitcoin was designed to operate on a decentralized, peer-to-peer network that uses blockchain technology to maintain a digital ledger of all transactions.

Bitcoin quickly gained popularity among enthusiasts who were attracted to its decentralized nature and the potential for anonymous transactions. As more people became interested in Bitcoin, the price of the cryptocurrency skyrocketed, reaching an all-time high of nearly $20,000 per Bitcoin in December 2017.

The success of Bitcoin spurred the creation of other cryptocurrencies, with thousands now available. Some of the most popular cryptocurrencies include Ethereum, Ripple, Litecoin, and Bitcoin Cash. Each cryptocurrency has its own unique features and benefits, and the cryptocurrency market continues to evolve rapidly.

While cryptocurrencies have gained a lot of attention and popularity in recent years, they have also faced significant challenges and setbacks. In 2014, for example, one of the largest Bitcoin exchanges, Mt. Gox, filed for bankruptcy after losing hundreds of millions of dollars worth of Bitcoin in a hack. Other high-profile incidents, such as the hack of the DAO (Decentralized Autonomous Organization) in 2016, have also raised concerns about the security of cryptocurrencies and the risks associated with investing in them.

Despite these challenges, the use of cryptocurrencies continues to grow, with more and more businesses starting to accept them as payment and investors becoming more interested in them as an alternative asset class. However, the lack of regulation and the high volatility of cryptocurrencies remain significant challenges, and it is still unclear what role cryptocurrencies will ultimately play in the future of finance.

In the following chapters of this book, we will explore some of the risks and challenges associated with cryptocurrencies, including their volatility, lack of regulation, security risks, environmental impact, lack of acceptance, and complex technology. By examining these issues, we hope to provide a comprehensive understanding of the potential risks and rewards of investing in cryptocurrencies.

Importance of discussing the downsides of cryptocurrencies

While cryptocurrencies have gained popularity and attention as a potentially disruptive technology, it is important to recognize that they are not without their downsides. In fact, it is essential to have an honest discussion about the risks and challenges associated with cryptocurrencies in order to make informed decisions about investing in them.

One of the primary reasons why it is important to discuss the downsides of cryptocurrencies is that they are a relatively new and untested technology. While the blockchain technology that underlies many cryptocurrencies is considered secure, it is not immune to hacking and other security risks. There have been several high-profile hacks and scams in the cryptocurrency space, which have resulted in significant losses for investors.

Another reason why it is important to discuss the downsides of cryptocurrencies is the lack of regulation in the space. Cryptocurrencies are not subject to the same regulatory oversight as traditional financial assets, which means that investors may not have the same legal protections and recourse in the event of fraud or other criminal activity.

In addition to security and regulatory concerns, cryptocurrencies also face challenges in terms of their environmental impact. The process of mining cryptocurrencies requires a significant amount of energy, which has raised concerns about their carbon footprint and sustainability.

Furthermore, the high volatility of cryptocurrencies is another issue that investors need to consider. Cryptocurrencies are known for their extreme price swings, which can lead to significant gains or losses in a short period of time. This volatility can make them a risky investment for those who are not prepared to handle the ups and downs of the market.

Ultimately, the importance of discussing the downsides of cryptocurrencies comes down to making informed investment decisions. By understanding the risks and challenges associated with cryptocurrencies, investors can make more informed decisions about whether or not to invest in them. This is particularly important for those who are new to the cryptocurrency space and may not be familiar with the risks involved.

In the following chapters of this book, we will delve into the six most significant downsides of cryptocurrencies, examining their impact on investors and the broader financial system. By doing so, we aim to provide readers with a comprehensive understanding of the potential risks and rewards of investing in cryptocurrencies.

Overview of the six bad things to be discussed in the book

In this book, we will take an in-depth look at six major downsides of cryptocurrencies, each of which has the potential to significantly impact investors and the broader financial system. These six bad things are:

Volatility: Cryptocurrencies are notorious for their volatility, with prices sometimes fluctuating by double-digit percentages in a matter of hours. This makes them a risky investment for those who are not prepared to handle the ups and downs of the market.

Security: Despite the use of blockchain technology, which is considered secure, cryptocurrencies are not immune to hacking and other security risks. There have been several high-profile hacks and scams in the cryptocurrency space, which have resulted in significant losses for investors.

Lack of regulation: Cryptocurrencies are not subject to the same regulatory oversight as traditional financial assets, which mean that investors may not have the same legal protections and recourse in the event of fraud or other criminal activity.

Environmental impact: The process of mining cryptocurrencies requires a significant amount of energy, which has raised concerns about their carbon footprint and sustainability.

Use in illegal activities: Cryptocurrencies have been associated with illegal activities such as money laundering and drug trafficking, which has led to increased scrutiny and regulation.

Speculative nature: Many investors see cryptocurrencies as a speculative investment rather than a true currency or store of value, which has led to price bubbles and crashes.

Each of these six bad things will be examined in detail in the following chapters, with a focus on their impact on investors and the broader financial system. By understanding these downsides, readers will be better equipped to make informed decisions about whether or not to invest in cryptocurrencies.

While the downsides of cryptocurrencies are significant, it is important to recognize that they are not the whole story. Cryptocurrencies also have the potential to revolutionize the financial system, providing greater access to financial services and reducing transaction costs. In order to fully understand the potential of cryptocurrencies, it is important to consider both their upsides and downsides.

Chapter 1: Volatility

Explanation of volatility in the cryptocurrency market

Volatility is a term used to describe the degree of variation of a financial asset's price over time. In the context of cryptocurrencies, volatility is a major concern for investors, as prices can fluctuate dramatically in a short period of time. This can lead to significant gains or losses for those who invest in the market.

There are several factors that contribute to the volatility of cryptocurrencies. One of the primary factors is the lack of intrinsic value. Unlike traditional assets such as stocks or real estate, which have underlying assets or cash flows that provide a basis for valuation, cryptocurrencies have no such intrinsic value. Instead, their value is determined purely by supply and demand in the market, which can fluctuate based on a variety of factors.

Another factor that contributes to the volatility of cryptocurrencies is their limited liquidity. While the cryptocurrency market has grown significantly in recent years, it is still relatively small compared to traditional financial markets. This means that a large order to buy or sell can have a significant impact on prices. In addition, the market is still largely dominated by retail investors, who may be more likely to make emotional or impulsive trading decisions based on news or rumors.

A third factor that contributes to the volatility of cryptocurrencies is their lack of regulatory oversight. While some jurisdictions have begun to introduce regulations for cryptocurrencies, the market remains largely unregulated. This means that there is no oversight or protection for investors, which can lead to wild swings in prices based on speculation or rumor.

Finally, the use of leverage and margin trading in the cryptocurrency market can also contribute to volatility. Leverage allows traders to increase their exposure to a particular asset by borrowing funds from a broker or exchange. While this can amplify potential gains, it can also magnify losses and increase volatility in the market.

Overall, the volatility of cryptocurrencies is a major concern for investors, particularly those who are not prepared to handle the ups and downs of the market. However, it is important to note that volatility is not necessarily a bad thing. In fact, it is often the volatility that attracts investors to the market in the first place, as it provides the potential for significant gains in a relatively short period of time. Nonetheless, investors should always be aware of the risks involved and be prepared to weather the ups and downs of the market.

Examples of extreme price fluctuations

As mentioned in the introduction, volatility is a major concern for investors in the cryptocurrency market. This is because prices can fluctuate dramatically in a short period of time, which can lead to significant gains or losses for those who invest in the market. In this section, we'll explore some examples of extreme price fluctuations in the cryptocurrency market to illustrate the potential risks and rewards of investing in this space.

One of the most well-known examples of extreme price fluctuations in the cryptocurrency market is the rise and fall of Bitcoin's price in 2017. In early 2017, the price of Bitcoin was around $1,000. By December of the same year, it had reached a peak of nearly $20,000. However, in the following months, the price dropped significantly, reaching a low of around $3,000 in late 2018. This represents a nearly 95% drop in value from its peak, and a significant loss for those who had invested at the peak.

Another example of extreme price fluctuations is the rise and fall of the cryptocurrency market as a whole in early 2018. In January of that year, the total market capitalization of all cryptocurrencies reached a peak of nearly $830 billion. However, by February of the same year, the market had crashed, with the total market capitalization dropping to around $280 billion. This represents a nearly 66% drop in value in just a few weeks, and a significant loss for those who had invested at the peak.

Other examples of extreme price fluctuations in the cryptocurrency market include the "flash crash" of Ethereum in 2017, where the price of Ethereum dropped from over $300 to just $0.10 in a matter of seconds before quickly recovering, and the "pump and dump" schemes that have been used to manipulate the price of various cryptocurrencies.

While extreme price fluctuations can be a major risk for investors, they can also provide opportunities for significant gains. For example, those who had invested in Bitcoin in the early days and held on to their investments through the volatility of the market would have seen significant gains in the long run. Similarly, those who were able to buy cryptocurrencies at the bottom of the market in 2018 would have seen significant gains as the market recovered in the following years.

Overall, the extreme price fluctuations in the cryptocurrency market highlight the potential risks and rewards of investing in this space. While the volatility can be a major concern for investors, it can also provide opportunities for significant gains for those who are able to navigate the market effectively.

Factors that contribute to volatility

Cryptocurrencies have been known for their extreme volatility, which is characterized by sudden and sharp price fluctuations. There are various factors that contribute to this volatility, which can be broadly classified into two categories: market-related and non-market-related factors.

Market-related factors that contribute to volatility include supply and demand dynamics, news events, and regulatory changes. The supply and demand of a particular cryptocurrency can be influenced by a variety of factors, such as the total number of coins in circulation, the rate at which new coins are mined or released, and the level of investor interest. Any changes in these factors can have a significant impact on the price of a cryptocurrency.

News events can also significantly impact the cryptocurrency market. Positive news, such as new partnerships or adoption by major companies, can cause a surge in demand, leading to an increase in price. On the other hand, negative news, such as regulatory crackdowns or security breaches, can cause panic selling and a sudden drop in price.

Regulatory changes can also contribute to volatility. Cryptocurrencies operate in a largely unregulated market, which means that any changes in regulations can have a significant impact on the market. For example, if a major country were to ban or severely restrict the use of cryptocurrencies, it could cause a sharp drop in demand, leading to a decrease in price.

Non-market-related factors that contribute to volatility include technological issues, security breaches, and manipulation. Technological issues, such as bugs or glitches in the code, can cause sudden and unpredictable price movements. Security breaches, such as the hacking of a major exchange or wallet, can also have a significant impact on the market. Manipulation, such as pump and dump schemes, can also contribute to volatility by artificially inflating or deflating the price of a particular cryptocurrency.

Overall, the cryptocurrency market is still in its early stages and is subject to significant volatility. While there are a number of factors that contribute to this volatility, many experts believe that as the market matures and becomes more widely adopted, volatility will gradually decrease.

Risks and Challenges for Investors

The extreme volatility of the cryptocurrency market can pose significant risks and challenges for investors. Here are some of the key risks and challenges that investors may face:

High Price Volatility: As we have discussed, the prices of cryptocurrencies can fluctuate rapidly and unpredictably. This means that investors can experience significant gains or losses in a short period of time. For some investors, this volatility can be too much to handle, and they may choose to exit the market altogether.

Liquidity Risks: Cryptocurrency exchanges can be illiquid, meaning that there may not be enough buyers or sellers to execute a trade. This can make it difficult to buy or sell a particular cryptocurrency at the desired price. In some cases, investors may be forced to sell at a lower price or hold on to a cryptocurrency that they cannot sell.

Cybersecurity Risks: The cryptocurrency market is susceptible to cyberattacks, including hacking, phishing, and ransomware attacks. Investors' wallets and exchanges are particularly vulnerable to these attacks, and investors can lose their investments if their cryptocurrency is stolen or hacked.

Regulatory Risks: The lack of regulatory oversight in the cryptocurrency market can pose a risk to investors. There is currently no uniform regulation of cryptocurrencies across jurisdictions, and some countries have banned or restricted the use of cryptocurrencies. The lack of regulation can create uncertainty and unpredictability in the market, making it difficult for investors to make informed decisions.

Technical Risks: The technology underlying cryptocurrencies is complex and can be difficult to understand. Investors who are not technically proficient may struggle to understand the underlying technology and may make poor investment decisions as a result.

In summary, the high volatility of the cryptocurrency market can pose significant risks and challenges for investors. As with any investment, it is important for investors to carefully consider the risks before investing in cryptocurrencies.

Chapter 2: Lack of Regulation
Explanation of the lack of regulation in the cryptocurrency market

The lack of regulation in the cryptocurrency market is a significant concern for investors and regulators alike. Unlike traditional financial markets, the cryptocurrency market operates with little to no oversight from government authorities or regulatory bodies. This lack of regulation has given rise to various challenges that pose a threat to investors' security and market stability.

One of the main reasons for the lack of regulation in the cryptocurrency market is the decentralized nature of cryptocurrencies. Unlike traditional financial institutions that operate under the purview of government regulators, cryptocurrencies are not backed by any centralized authority. This makes it difficult for regulators to monitor transactions and track illegal activities, such as money laundering and terrorist financing.

Another factor contributing to the lack of regulation in the cryptocurrency market is the novelty of the technology. Cryptocurrencies and blockchain technology are still relatively new, and regulatory bodies have been slow to adapt to this rapidly evolving landscape. The lack of clear guidelines and regulations has created uncertainty for investors and slowed the adoption of cryptocurrencies in traditional financial markets.

Moreover, there is a lack of consensus among governments and regulatory bodies regarding how to classify and regulate cryptocurrencies. Some governments have taken a more hands-on approach, while others have been more hesitant, preferring to wait and watch how the market develops. This lack of uniformity in regulations has created an inconsistent and confusing regulatory environment for investors and businesses alike.

Overall, the lack of regulation in the cryptocurrency market is a significant challenge that needs to be addressed. As cryptocurrencies continue to gain mainstream adoption, it's essential for regulators to provide clear guidelines and regulations to protect investors and promote market stability. The next section will explore the implications of this lack of regulation and the potential solutions to address it.

Examples of fraudulent and illegal activities involving cryptocurrencies

The lack of regulation in the cryptocurrency market has created a breeding ground for fraudulent and illegal activities. Because of the anonymous and decentralized nature of cryptocurrencies, it can be difficult to trace transactions and hold bad actors accountable. In this section, we will explore some of the most notable examples of fraud and illegal activity involving cryptocurrencies.

One of the most well-known examples of fraud in the cryptocurrency market is the case of OneCoin. OneCoin was a multi-level marketing scheme that claimed to be a cryptocurrency, but in reality, it was a pyramid scheme that bilked investors out of billions of dollars. OneCoin's leaders created a fake cryptocurrency and used aggressive marketing tactics to convince people to invest in it. They promised huge returns and even held events where investors could purchase OneCoin packages for thousands of dollars. However, the OneCoin cryptocurrency was not publicly traded, had no real value, and was not recognized by any legitimate cryptocurrency exchange. In 2017, the scheme was exposed, and its leaders were indicted on charges of wire fraud, securities fraud, and money laundering.

Another example of fraudulent activity in the cryptocurrency market is the case of BitConnect. BitConnect was a lending and exchange platform that promised investors returns of up to 40% per month. However, the platform was a Ponzi scheme that relied on new investors to pay off earlier investors. When the platform eventually collapsed, investors lost millions of dollars. The Securities and Exchange Commission (SEC) has since filed charges against the individuals behind BitConnect.

Cryptocurrencies have also been used to facilitate illegal activities such as money laundering and the purchase of illegal goods and services. One notorious example is the Silk Road marketplace, an online platform that facilitated the sale of illegal drugs and other illicit goods. Transactions on the Silk Road were conducted using Bitcoin, which allowed buyers and sellers to remain anonymous. The marketplace was shut down in 2013, and its founder, Ross Ulbricht, was sentenced to life in prison.

In addition to these high-profile cases, there have been countless smaller-scale examples of fraud and illegal activity in the cryptocurrency market. Scammers have created fake ICOs (initial coin offerings) to bilk investors out of their money, while hackers have stolen millions of dollars' worth of cryptocurrencies from exchanges and wallets. The lack of regulation in the market makes it easier for bad actors to get away with these activities and puts investors at risk.

In conclusion, the lack of regulation in the cryptocurrency market has led to numerous examples of fraud and illegal activity. Investors must be cautious when investing in cryptocurrencies and do their due diligence to ensure that they are not falling victim to a scam. Governments and regulatory bodies must also step up their efforts to provide oversight and protect investors in this emerging market.

Potential risks for investors and the market as a whole

While the lack of regulation in the cryptocurrency market has provided certain benefits such as anonymity, flexibility, and accessibility, it has also resulted in numerous risks and challenges for investors and the market as a whole. One of the primary risks associated with the absence of regulations is the potential for fraudulent and illegal activities.

Without clear guidelines and oversight, bad actors can exploit the lack of regulation to engage in activities such as market manipulation, theft, money laundering, and scams. This can significantly harm investors, destabilize the market, and erode trust in the overall cryptocurrency ecosystem.

In addition to fraudulent and illegal activities, there are other potential risks for investors in the absence of regulations. For example, there is a risk that cryptocurrency exchanges could go out of business, leading to the loss of investors' funds. There is also a risk of technological failure or cyber-attacks, which can result in the loss of digital assets.

The lack of regulatory oversight also means that there is no clear mechanism for resolving disputes, enforcing contracts, or protecting investors from market volatility. This lack of protection and legal recourse can make it challenging for investors to feel confident in the market and can limit participation from more risk-averse investors.

Furthermore, the lack of regulation in the cryptocurrency market can also pose a risk to the market as a whole. As the market grows and attracts more investors, it becomes more susceptible to large-scale disruptions and systemic risks. These risks can have a cascading effect on the broader financial system, particularly if they are left unchecked.

In summary, the lack of regulation in the cryptocurrency market creates a range of potential risks and challenges for investors and the market as a whole. It is essential for regulators to strike a balance between supporting innovation and protecting investors and the broader financial system.

Current State of Regulation and Future Prospects

The cryptocurrency market is largely unregulated, and this has led to several concerns regarding consumer protection and market integrity. As a result, there is a growing interest in regulating the market to ensure that investors are protected and that the industry is not being used for illegal activities.

At present, the regulation of cryptocurrencies is still in its early stages. Some countries have taken steps to regulate the market, but there is no uniform approach to regulation globally. Some countries, such as Japan, have passed legislation that recognizes cryptocurrencies as a legal payment method, while other countries, such as China, have banned cryptocurrencies altogether.

In the United States, the Securities and Exchange Commission (SEC) has taken an active role in regulating the cryptocurrency market. The SEC has declared that cryptocurrencies are securities and subject to federal securities laws, and it has taken action against several fraudulent initial coin offerings (ICOs). However, the regulation of cryptocurrencies is still a complex and evolving issue, and there is no clear regulatory framework in place.

One of the main challenges with regulating cryptocurrencies is that they are global in nature and not tied to any specific country or jurisdiction. This makes it difficult for regulators to enforce regulations, particularly in cases where the cryptocurrency is being used for illegal activities.

Despite these challenges, there are several efforts underway to regulate the cryptocurrency market. In the United States, for example, there are ongoing discussions about the need for a regulatory framework for cryptocurrencies. Some proponents have suggested that a regulatory sandbox approach could be taken, which would allow for experimentation with new regulatory approaches without imposing overly burdensome regulations.

In Europe, the European Union has taken steps to regulate the cryptocurrency market, with the fifth anti-money laundering directive (AMLD5) coming into effect in January 2020. The AMLD5 requires cryptocurrency exchanges and wallet providers to perform due diligence on their customers and report any suspicious transactions to the relevant authorities.

Looking to the future, it is likely that the regulation of cryptocurrencies will continue to evolve and become more comprehensive. Regulators will need to balance the need to protect consumers and maintain market integrity with the desire to foster innovation in the industry. It is also likely that there will be continued debate over the appropriate level of regulation and whether a global regulatory framework is needed.

Overall, while the regulation of cryptocurrencies is still in its early stages, there are indications that more comprehensive regulation is on the horizon. This could help to address some of the downsides of cryptocurrencies, such as fraud and lack of consumer protection, and make the industry more accessible to mainstream investors.

Chapter 3: Security Risks
Explanation of the security risks associated with cryptocurrencies

Cryptocurrencies are decentralized digital currencies that are built on complex cryptographic algorithms and operate on distributed ledger technology known as the blockchain. While this innovative technology has opened up new opportunities for financial transactions, it also poses a significant security risk for investors and traders.

One of the primary security risks associated with cryptocurrencies is the possibility of hacking attacks. As digital assets, cryptocurrencies are stored in digital wallets, which are typically secured with private keys. However, if a hacker gains access to an individual's private key, they can easily steal their cryptocurrencies, resulting in significant financial losses.

Another security risk is the potential for fraud in the form of Ponzi schemes, fake ICOs, and other scams. With little to no regulatory oversight, it is easy for unscrupulous individuals to set up fraudulent schemes and mislead investors into buying into them. Additionally, cryptocurrency exchanges have been hacked in the past, leading to massive losses for investors.

Phishing attacks and social engineering are also prevalent in the cryptocurrency space, with hackers impersonating exchanges or popular cryptocurrency figures to trick individuals into revealing their private keys or other sensitive information.

Moreover, the pseudonymous nature of cryptocurrencies makes it a haven for criminal activities such as money laundering, drug trafficking, and other illegal activities. Criminals use cryptocurrencies as a way to evade law enforcement and operate anonymously, making it difficult for authorities to track their activities.

Overall, the security risks associated with cryptocurrencies are significant and should be carefully considered by anyone investing in them. Investors should take proactive steps to secure their digital wallets and exercise caution when engaging in cryptocurrency transactions.

Types of cyberattacks targeting cryptocurrency exchanges and wallets

In recent years, the security risks associated with cryptocurrencies have become a major concern for investors and enthusiasts alike. One of the most significant security risks in the cryptocurrency market is the prevalence of cyberattacks targeting cryptocurrency exchanges and wallets.

Cryptocurrency exchanges and wallets are online platforms where investors can buy, sell, and store their digital assets. These platforms have become a primary target for cybercriminals due to the significant amounts of money and valuable digital assets that are stored within them.

There are several types of cyberattacks that target cryptocurrency exchanges and wallets, including phishing attacks, malware attacks, and distributed denial of service (DDoS) attacks.

Phishing attacks are a common tactic used by cybercriminals to gain access to investors' cryptocurrency accounts. In a phishing attack, cybercriminals will send fraudulent emails or messages that mimic legitimate communications from cryptocurrency exchanges or wallets. These messages often include links to fake websites that look identical to legitimate exchanges or wallets. Once an investor enters their login credentials into these fake websites, cybercriminals can use this information to gain access to their accounts and steal their digital assets.

Malware attacks are another common tactic used by cybercriminals to steal cryptocurrencies. In a malware attack, cybercriminals will install malicious software onto an investor's device, such as a computer or smartphone. This software can then be used to gain access to the investor's cryptocurrency accounts, steal their login credentials, and steal their digital assets.

DDoS attacks are a third type of cyberattack that can be used to target cryptocurrency exchanges and wallets. In a DDoS attack, cybercriminals will flood the exchange or wallet's servers with an overwhelming amount of traffic, causing the platform to become overwhelmed and crash. This can prevent investors from accessing their accounts, which can cause panic and uncertainty in the market.

In addition to these types of attacks, there are other security risks associated with cryptocurrency exchanges and wallets. For example, there is always the risk that an exchange or wallet could be hacked and that investors' digital assets could be stolen. There is also the risk that an exchange or wallet could be shut down or seized by authorities, which could result in investors losing their digital assets.

Overall, the security risks associated with cryptocurrency exchanges and wallets are a significant concern for investors and the market as a whole. As the market continues to grow, it is important for investors to take steps to protect their digital assets and for cryptocurrency exchanges and wallets to take steps to improve their security measures.

Best practices for securing cryptocurrencies

As discussed in the previous sections, security is a major concern when it comes to dealing with cryptocurrencies. To protect their digital assets, investors need to take proactive measures to secure their wallets and protect themselves from malicious attacks. This section will discuss some of the best practices for securing cryptocurrencies.

Use a Hardware Wallet

Hardware wallets are considered the most secure option for storing cryptocurrencies. They are physical devices that store the private keys used to access and manage a cryptocurrency wallet. Unlike online wallets, which are vulnerable to hacking, hardware wallets are offline and cannot be accessed remotely.

Keep Private Keys Offline

Investors should keep their private keys offline and in a secure location. Private keys are the means of accessing a cryptocurrency wallet and managing its contents. If a private key falls into the wrong hands, the wallet can be easily compromised. By keeping private keys offline, investors can reduce the risk of theft or loss.

Use Two-Factor Authentication

Two-factor authentication (2FA) is a security measure that requires users to provide two forms of identification to access an account. 2FA can be used to secure online wallets and exchanges. When enabled, a user will need to provide a password and a second form of identification, such as a code sent to their phone, to access their account. This makes it much harder for hackers to gain unauthorized access.

Keep Software Up to Date

Cryptocurrency software is constantly evolving, and developers regularly release updates to patch vulnerabilities and improve security. It is important to keep cryptocurrency software up to date to ensure that known vulnerabilities are patched and new security features are implemented.

Back Up Your Wallet

Investors should regularly back up their cryptocurrency wallet to ensure that they can recover their funds if their wallet is lost or compromised. Backups can be stored in multiple locations to reduce the risk of loss or theft.

Be Cautious of Phishing Scams

Phishing scams are a common tactic used by hackers to gain access to sensitive information, including private keys and account credentials. These scams typically involve the use of fake websites or emails that mimic legitimate sites or services. Investors should be cautious of any emails or messages that ask for personal information or direct them to a login page.

Use Secure Networks

When accessing cryptocurrency accounts or wallets, it is important to use secure networks. Public Wi-Fi networks and other unsecured connections can be vulnerable to hacking and may provide an entry point for attackers. It is recommended that investors only use secure, trusted networks to access their cryptocurrency accounts.

Diversify Your Investments

Investors should consider diversifying their cryptocurrency holdings to reduce the impact of a potential security breach. By holding multiple cryptocurrencies, investors can reduce the risk of losing all their digital assets in a single attack.

In conclusion, securing cryptocurrencies requires a combination of best practices, including the use of hardware wallets, two-factor authentication, keeping software up to date, backing up wallets, and using secure networks. While there is no foolproof method for securing cryptocurrencies, following these practices can significantly reduce the risk of loss or theft.

Best Practices	Description	Recommended Tools/Utilities/Devices
1. Store Cryptocurrencies Offline	Keeping cryptocurrencies offline in hardware wallets, paper wallets, or other secure physical storage can protect	Ledger Nano S, Trezor, KeepKey
2. Use Strong Passwords and Multifactor Authentication	Strong passwords that are unique for each account, as well as multifactor authentication (such as	LastPass, Authy, Google Authenticator, YubiKey
3. Keep Software Up to Date	Regularly updating software, including operating systems and wallets, can fix vulnerabilities and improve	Automatic update features, such as those in operating systems and wallet software
4. Be Cautious of Phishing Attempts	Phishing emails, messages, or websites can trick users into giving away their private keys or login credentials. Users	Antiphishing software, such as Avast or McAfee, or a hardware security key
5. Use Decentralized Exchanges	Decentralized exchanges (DEXs) allow users to trade cryptocurrencies without the need for a central authority,	Uniswap, PancakeSwap, Sushiswap
6. Backup Private Keys and Seed Phrases	Private keys and seed phrases should be backed up and stored securely in case of loss or theft.	Password-protected encrypted external hard drives or cloud storage services, such as Dropbox or Google Drive

This table provides a clear and organized way for readers to understand the best practices for securing cryptocurrencies and the recommended tools, utilities, or devices to implement them.

Future developments in cryptocurrency security

As the cryptocurrency market continues to evolve, so too do the methods used to secure these digital assets. Despite the many security risks that exist in the cryptocurrency space, there is also a growing industry dedicated to creating new solutions to these problems. In this section, we will explore some of the most promising developments in cryptocurrency security and what the future of digital asset protection may look like.

Multi-Factor Authentication: One of the most promising developments in cryptocurrency security is the use of multi-factor authentication. This involves using more than one method to verify a user's identity when accessing their digital assets, such as a password and a biometric identifier like a fingerprint. This approach can greatly reduce the risk of unauthorized access to a user's wallet or exchange account.

Hardware Wallets: Hardware wallets are physical devices that store a user's private keys offline, making them much more difficult to hack. These devices can be used to store a wide range of cryptocurrencies, and many of them have built-in security features like PIN codes and two-factor authentication. As hardware wallets become more widespread, they are likely to become a go-to solution for users looking to secure their digital assets.

Decentralized Exchanges: Another promising development in cryptocurrency security is the rise of decentralized exchanges. These are exchanges that operate on a peer-to-peer network rather than through a centralized authority, making them much more difficult to hack. Decentralized exchanges also eliminate many of the risks associated with centralization, such as the potential for a single point of failure.

Blockchain Analysis Tools: As the cryptocurrency market has grown, so too has the industry dedicated to analyzing blockchain data. There are now a wide range of tools and services available to help users track the movement of their digital assets and identify potential security risks. These tools can be used to monitor transactions, identify suspicious activity, and more.

Smart Contract Auditing: One of the biggest risks associated with the use of smart contracts is the potential for bugs or vulnerabilities that could be exploited by attackers. To mitigate this risk, there has been a growing industry dedicated to auditing smart contracts to identify potential issues before they can be exploited. This is likely to become an increasingly important part of the cryptocurrency security landscape as the use of smart contracts continues to grow.

Overall, there are many exciting developments in the cryptocurrency security space, and it is likely that we will continue to see new solutions emerge as the market evolves. While there will always be risks associated with digital assets, there are also many promising technologies and approaches that can be used to mitigate these risks and keep users' assets secure. By staying up-to-date on the latest developments in this space and following best practices for securing their digital assets, cryptocurrency users can help ensure that their investments remain safe and secure.

Future Development	Description	Potential Benefits
Hardware Wallets	Continued development of secure hardware wallets with enhanced features and capabilities	Increased security of private keys and protection against physical attacks
Multi-Signature Wallets	Increased adoption of multi-signature wallets that require multiple signatures for transactions	Improved protection against theft and fraud
Decentralized Exchanges	Greater adoption of decentralized exchanges that do not rely on a central authority or point of failure	Enhanced security and privacy for users
Privacy Coins	The development and adoption of privacy-focused cryptocurrencies that protect user identities and transaction	Improved privacy and security for users
Quantum-Resistant Cryptography	The development and implementation of quantum-resistant cryptography to protect against future threats	Enhanced long-term security for the cryptocurrency ecosystem
Improved Regulatory Frameworks	The development of clear and effective regulatory frameworks that protect investors and promote	Increased trust and confidence in the cryptocurrency market

Note that this is just one possible table and that there are many other future developments that could be included as well.

Chapter 4: Environmental Impact
Explanation of the environmental impact of cryptocurrency mining

Cryptocurrency mining, the process of validating transactions on the blockchain and earning newly minted coins as a reward, has been criticized for its environmental impact. This impact is largely due to the high energy consumption required by mining operations, which has led to concerns over carbon emissions and the potential contribution to climate change.

The environmental impact of cryptocurrency mining can be explained by examining the process and requirements of mining itself. In order to successfully mine cryptocurrencies, specialized hardware and software must be used to solve complex mathematical problems. This process is called Proof of Work (PoW), which is used by many popular cryptocurrencies such as Bitcoin and Ethereum. PoW requires miners to compete with each other to solve the mathematical problems, which consumes a significant amount of energy.

The energy consumption associated with mining cryptocurrencies is due to the fact that the mathematical problems that need to be solved are very difficult and require a lot of computational power. This computational power is provided by specialized hardware, such as Application-Specific Integrated Circuits (ASICs) and Graphics Processing Units (GPUs), which are designed to perform these calculations quickly and efficiently. However, the high energy consumption of this specialized hardware has led to concerns over the environmental impact of cryptocurrency mining.

One of the main ways that cryptocurrency mining contributes to environmental damage is through the energy sources used to power mining operations. The majority of the world's electricity is generated from non-renewable sources, such as coal and natural gas. When this electricity is used to power mining operations, it contributes to carbon emissions and other forms of pollution. This has led to concerns over the impact of mining on climate change and the need for alternative, more sustainable energy sources to power mining operations.

Another factor that contributes to the environmental impact of cryptocurrency mining is the e-waste generated by the specialized hardware used in mining operations. ASICs and GPUs are not recyclable and often end up in landfills, where they can leach toxic chemicals into the environment. The production and disposal of these mining devices can also lead to other environmental problems, such as water and air pollution.

In addition to the environmental impact of mining operations, there are also concerns over the impact of the cryptocurrency industry as a whole. The growing popularity of cryptocurrencies has led to an increase in demand for energy, as well as an increase in the amount of e-waste generated. This has led to calls for the industry to take greater responsibility for its environmental impact and to develop more sustainable practices.

As the environmental impact of cryptocurrency mining has become more widely recognized, there have been efforts to address these issues. One approach is to switch from PoW to alternative consensus mechanisms, such as Proof of Stake (PoS) or Proof of Authority (PoA), which require significantly less energy consumption. Another approach is to use renewable energy sources to power mining operations, such as solar or wind power. Additionally, some mining operations have implemented recycling and disposal programs for their e-waste.

While there are ongoing efforts to reduce the environmental impact of cryptocurrency mining, it remains a significant concern for the industry and for society as a whole. As the popularity and adoption of cryptocurrencies continues to grow, it will be important to address these environmental challenges in a sustainable and responsible manner.

Comparison of energy consumption of cryptocurrency mining to traditional financial systems

Cryptocurrency mining has been linked to significant energy consumption and its potential environmental impact has been a growing concern. To better understand this impact, it is important to compare the energy consumption of cryptocurrency mining to that of traditional financial systems.

Traditional financial systems, such as banks and credit card companies, are centralized and use electronic systems to process and verify transactions. These systems are generally considered to be more energy-efficient than cryptocurrency mining, as they require less computational power.

In contrast, cryptocurrency mining is a decentralized process that relies on solving complex mathematical problems to verify and process transactions on the blockchain. This process requires large amounts of computing power, which in turn requires significant energy consumption.

Recent studies have estimated the energy consumption of Bitcoin mining, the most popular cryptocurrency, to be around 110 terawatt-hours (TWh) per year, which is roughly equivalent to the energy consumption of small countries like Argentina or Sweden. This high energy consumption is due to the use of powerful computer equipment that runs continuously to maintain the blockchain network.

In comparison, traditional financial systems are estimated to use around 650 TWh per year, which includes the energy consumption of data centers, office buildings, and other infrastructure. While this is a significantly larger amount of energy consumption than cryptocurrency mining, it is important to note that these systems support a much larger economy and a greater volume of transactions.

Despite this, there are concerns about the environmental impact of cryptocurrency mining, particularly as the popularity of cryptocurrencies continues to grow. Some countries, such as China, have taken steps to limit the energy consumption of cryptocurrency mining by placing restrictions on mining operations or moving to renewable energy sources.

However, it is important to note that not all cryptocurrencies have the same level of energy consumption as Bitcoin. Some newer cryptocurrencies, such as Ethereum, have implemented energy-efficient mining algorithms that consume less energy than Bitcoin's mining process.

In summary, while the energy consumption of cryptocurrency mining is significant and has raised concerns about its environmental impact, it is important to compare this to the energy consumption of traditional financial systems. While traditional financial systems use more energy overall, they support a larger economy and a greater volume of transactions. As cryptocurrencies continue to evolve, it is important to consider the potential impact of these systems on the environment and to explore ways to reduce their energy consumption.

Comparison of Energy Consumption	Cryptocurrency Mining	Traditional Financial Systems
Energy consumption per transaction	Varies widely depending on the type of cryptocurrency and mining process, but can range from 600 kWh to 18,000 kWh	Much lower, estimated at about 0.01 kWh per transaction
Energy consumption per unit of value	Also varies widely, but can be as high as 800 kWh per Bitcoin	Much lower, estimated at about 0.1 kWh per $100 of transaction value
Total annual energy consumption	Estimated to be around 121.36 TWh as of May 2021	Not available, but likely much lower due to the centralized nature of traditional financial systems
Environmental impact	Significant, with mining contributing to carbon emissions and e-waste generation	Less significant, with the use of renewable energy sources and the more centralized nature of traditional financial systems

Note: The values presented in this table are only examples and may vary depending on the specific cryptocurrencies and financial systems being compared.

The carbon footprint of cryptocurrency mining

The carbon footprint of cryptocurrency mining is a growing concern in the industry, as the environmental impact of mining activities has become increasingly apparent. Cryptocurrency mining is a power-intensive process that requires massive amounts of electricity to perform the complex calculations necessary to verify transactions and create new blocks in the blockchain.

One of the primary sources of carbon emissions associated with cryptocurrency mining is the generation of electricity from fossil fuels. In many countries, the majority of electricity is still generated from coal-fired power plants, which are among the dirtiest sources of energy in terms of carbon emissions. The amount of carbon emissions associated with mining a single Bitcoin can be as high as 63 metric tons, according to some estimates.

The carbon footprint of cryptocurrency mining has become a significant concern for environmentalists, as it contributes to global warming and climate change. The amount of carbon emissions associated with mining a single Bitcoin is equivalent to the carbon emissions generated by driving a car for over 1 million miles. As the popularity of cryptocurrencies continues to grow, so too does the amount of energy required to mine them, which in turn leads to higher carbon emissions and a larger carbon footprint.

In addition to the environmental impact, the high energy consumption of cryptocurrency mining also has economic implications. The cost of electricity is a significant factor in the profitability of mining, and miners are constantly seeking the cheapest sources of energy in order to remain competitive. This has led to a concentration of mining activities in countries with low electricity costs, such as China, which generates a significant portion of its electricity from coal-fired power plants.

To address the environmental concerns associated with cryptocurrency mining, several initiatives have been launched to promote the use of renewable energy sources. Some mining operations have begun using solar or wind power to generate electricity, while others have experimented with utilizing excess energy from sources like hydropower. Additionally, some cryptocurrencies have been developed with a lower energy footprint in mind, such as Proof of Stake (PoS) cryptocurrencies, which require significantly less energy to operate than the traditional Proof of Work (PoW) model used by Bitcoin and other cryptocurrencies.

As the world becomes increasingly focused on sustainability and reducing carbon emissions, the environmental impact of cryptocurrency mining will continue to be a significant concern. It is important for the industry to explore new technologies and strategies to reduce energy consumption and carbon emissions, while still maintaining the security and integrity of the blockchain.

Potential solutions to reduce the environmental impact

Cryptocurrency mining has been criticized for its significant environmental impact, particularly in terms of energy consumption and carbon footprint. In response to this, researchers, policymakers, and industry players are exploring various potential solutions to mitigate the environmental impact of cryptocurrency mining.

One potential solution is the development of more energy-efficient mining hardware. Cryptocurrency mining hardware has evolved rapidly, with newer and more advanced models being developed that are more energy-efficient than their predecessors. For example, some newer models of Bitcoin mining machines use up to 50% less electricity than older models.

Another potential solution is the use of renewable energy sources to power cryptocurrency mining operations. Many cryptocurrency mining operations are currently powered by fossil fuels, which contribute significantly to carbon emissions. By using renewable energy sources such as solar or wind power, mining operations could reduce their environmental impact.

Some mining operations have already started using renewable energy sources, with some estimates suggesting that up to 70% of Bitcoin mining in China is powered by renewable energy sources such as hydropower. However, the use of renewable energy sources for mining is not without its challenges, as mining operations require a large amount of electricity that can be difficult to generate through renewable sources alone.

In addition to these technological solutions, there are also policy and regulatory approaches that could help reduce the environmental impact of cryptocurrency mining. For example, some jurisdictions have imposed taxes or fees on cryptocurrency mining operations based on their energy consumption or carbon emissions.

Another potential policy solution is the implementation of carbon credits or offsets for cryptocurrency mining. This would involve cryptocurrency miners buying and retiring carbon credits or investing in renewable energy projects to offset their carbon emissions.

Some experts have also proposed the development of decentralized, sustainable mining networks that use excess energy from renewable energy sources. These networks would use blockchain technology to connect renewable energy producers with cryptocurrency miners, enabling miners to access excess energy at lower prices and reducing the environmental impact of mining.

Finally, there is also a role for consumers and investors in reducing the environmental impact of cryptocurrency mining. By choosing to support cryptocurrencies that use more sustainable mining practices, consumers and investors can help to promote the adoption of more environmentally friendly practices in the industry.

In summary, there are various potential solutions to reduce the environmental impact of cryptocurrency mining. These include the development of more energy-efficient mining hardware, the use of renewable energy sources, policy and regulatory approaches, the development of sustainable mining networks, and consumer and investor choices. By pursuing a combination of these solutions, it may be possible to mitigate the environmental impact of cryptocurrency mining and promote a more sustainable future for the industry.

Chapter 5: Lack of Acceptance
Explanation of the limited acceptance of cryptocurrencies in mainstream society

Cryptocurrencies have been around for over a decade, but their adoption in mainstream society has been limited. Despite the growing number of businesses accepting cryptocurrencies as a form of payment, the overall acceptance is still low. This lack of acceptance can be attributed to a variety of factors, including the lack of awareness, the absence of regulatory frameworks, and the volatility of cryptocurrencies.

One of the main reasons for the limited acceptance of cryptocurrencies is the lack of awareness among the general public. Many people do not understand the concept of cryptocurrencies, how they work, or how to use them. As a result, they are hesitant to adopt this new form of currency. Additionally, the lack of clear regulations for cryptocurrencies can be a significant barrier to adoption. This ambiguity can make it difficult for businesses to comply with legal requirements and could leave them vulnerable to legal repercussions.

Another significant factor that limits the acceptance of cryptocurrencies is their volatility. Cryptocurrencies are known for their rapid price fluctuations, which can make it difficult for businesses to accept them as a form of payment. Because the value of cryptocurrencies can change so quickly, businesses may be reluctant to accept them as payment, as they may not be able to convert them into traditional currencies without experiencing significant losses.

Furthermore, the lack of infrastructure for cryptocurrencies can also be a significant barrier to their acceptance. While there are a growing number of businesses accepting cryptocurrencies, there are still many that do not. For example, it can be challenging to find physical locations that accept cryptocurrencies, and it can be even more challenging to use cryptocurrencies to pay for everyday goods and services.

Despite these challenges, there are several promising developments that could lead to increased acceptance of cryptocurrencies in the future. One of the most significant potential drivers of adoption is the growing popularity of decentralized finance (DeFi) platforms. DeFi platforms are built on blockchain technology and allow users to access a range of financial services without the need for traditional financial intermediaries. As DeFi platforms continue to gain popularity, it is likely that cryptocurrencies will become more widely accepted.

Moreover, the development of stablecoins, which are cryptocurrencies that are pegged to a stable asset such as a traditional currency or a commodity, could also increase acceptance. Stablecoins offer the benefits of cryptocurrencies, such as fast and inexpensive transactions, while also providing a level of stability that traditional cryptocurrencies lack.

Finally, the increasing interest and involvement of institutional investors in the cryptocurrency market could also lead to increased acceptance. As more traditional financial institutions begin to invest in cryptocurrencies, they may become more comfortable with the technology, which could lead to increased adoption and acceptance in mainstream society.

In summary, the limited acceptance of cryptocurrencies in mainstream society can be attributed to a variety of factors, including lack of awareness, absence of regulatory frameworks, volatility, and lack of infrastructure. However, there are promising developments, such as the growing popularity of DeFi platforms, the development of stablecoins, and the involvement of institutional investors, that could lead to increased adoption and acceptance in the future.

Challenge	Explanation	Possible Solutions
Complexity	Cryptocurrencies can be difficult to understand and use for the average person.	Develop user-friendly interfaces and educational resources for beginners. Increase awareness through marketing and public relations efforts.
Volatility	The price of cryptocurrencies can be highly volatile, making them risky for investors and difficult to use as a medium of exchange.	Develop stablecoins that are pegged to a fiat currency or basket of assets. Improve market liquidity and stability through regulation and increased adoption.
Trust	Cryptocurrencies are not backed by a central authority and are seen as risky or unstable by some.	Develop trust by increasing security and reducing fraud. Increase transparency and accountability through regulation and auditable financial statements.
Integration	Cryptocurrencies are not widely accepted by merchants and are not yet integrated into traditional financial systems.	Increase adoption by incentivizing merchants to accept cryptocurrencies. Develop partnerships with financial institutions and integrate cryptocurrencies into existing financial infrastructure.
Perception	Cryptocurrencies are often associated with illicit activities and scams, leading to a negative perception in the mainstream.	Improve education and public relations efforts to increase awareness and understanding of the legitimate use cases for cryptocurrencies. Increase enforcement of regulations to reduce illicit activities and scams.

This table is not exhaustive and there may be other challenges and solutions not included. Additionally, some solutions may overlap with multiple challenges.

Reasons why businesses are hesitant to accept cryptocurrencies

Despite the growing popularity and adoption of cryptocurrencies, many businesses remain hesitant to accept them as a form of payment. There are several reasons why this is the case. First, the volatility of cryptocurrencies is a major concern for businesses. Cryptocurrencies such as Bitcoin can experience significant price fluctuations in short periods of time, making it difficult for businesses to determine the value of their holdings. This can create significant accounting and tax reporting challenges for businesses, which may deter them from accepting cryptocurrencies.

Second, there are concerns about the regulatory environment surrounding cryptocurrencies. Because cryptocurrencies are not yet widely accepted or regulated by governments, businesses may be hesitant to accept them for fear of running afoul of regulatory requirements. There is also the issue of legal liability, as businesses may be held responsible for any illicit activities that are conducted using cryptocurrencies.

Third, there are technological barriers to accepting cryptocurrencies. Many businesses may not have the necessary infrastructure or expertise to accept cryptocurrencies as a form of payment. This can include issues related to security and data privacy, as well as the need for specialized hardware or software to facilitate cryptocurrency transactions.

Fourth, there is a lack of consumer demand for cryptocurrencies as a payment method. Although the popularity of cryptocurrencies has grown in recent years, they are still not widely used or understood by the general public. This can make it difficult for businesses to justify the investment in time and resources necessary to implement cryptocurrency payment systems.

Finally, there is the issue of usability. Cryptocurrencies can be complex and confusing for the average user, and the process of setting up a cryptocurrency wallet and making transactions can be time-consuming and cumbersome. This can create a significant barrier to adoption, especially for businesses that rely on quick and easy payment processing.

Overall, there are many reasons why businesses are hesitant to accept cryptocurrencies, including concerns about volatility, regulation, technology, consumer demand, and usability. Addressing these challenges will be essential to increasing acceptance and adoption of cryptocurrencies in mainstream society.

Efforts to increase acceptance and adoption

Efforts to increase acceptance and adoption of cryptocurrencies have been ongoing since their inception, as the potential benefits of this technology continue to be realized. While there is still a lack of acceptance of cryptocurrencies in mainstream society, there are various efforts underway to increase adoption and use.

One major area of focus has been increasing awareness and education about cryptocurrencies. As the general public becomes more informed about the technology and its potential benefits, it may be more likely to accept and use cryptocurrencies. Efforts to increase awareness and education include creating online courses, publishing articles and whitepapers, and holding seminars and conferences.

Another approach to increasing acceptance and adoption of cryptocurrencies is through increased regulatory clarity. Many businesses and individuals are hesitant to adopt cryptocurrencies due to regulatory uncertainty and concerns about legal compliance. Governments and regulatory bodies are increasingly developing guidelines and regulations for cryptocurrencies, which can help provide greater clarity and reduce the perceived risk.

In addition to awareness, education, and regulatory clarity, there are also efforts to increase the accessibility and usability of cryptocurrencies. This includes developing easier-to-use wallets, improving user interfaces, and expanding the range of businesses that accept cryptocurrencies as payment.

Furthermore, some organizations are working to create stablecoins, which are cryptocurrencies that are pegged to the value of an underlying asset such as the US dollar. Stablecoins are seen as a way to reduce the volatility that has been a major concern for many businesses and individuals considering using cryptocurrencies.

Finally, there are efforts to improve the security and scalability of cryptocurrencies. Security concerns have been a major barrier to adoption, and improving security measures can increase confidence in the technology. Additionally, scaling issues such as high transaction fees and slow processing times have been a major hindrance to adoption, and efforts are underway to address these challenges through the development of new technologies such as the Lightning Network.

Overall, there are various efforts underway to increase acceptance and adoption of cryptocurrencies. By increasing awareness, improving regulatory clarity, increasing accessibility and usability, developing stablecoins, and improving security and scalability, it is hoped that the benefits of cryptocurrencies can be more widely realized.

Future outlook for cryptocurrency as a practical currency

As cryptocurrencies continue to gain mainstream attention, the question remains: will they become a practical currency for everyday use in the future?

Currently, many experts believe that widespread adoption of cryptocurrencies as a practical currency is still a ways off. One of the main reasons for this is the lack of stability and volatility of cryptocurrency prices. The value of cryptocurrencies can fluctuate widely in a short period of time, making it difficult for consumers to use them as a stable means of exchange.

Another issue that needs to be addressed is the scalability of cryptocurrencies. As more people use cryptocurrencies, the networks that support them will need to be able to handle increased transaction volumes. However, many cryptocurrencies are not yet equipped to handle the same transaction volumes as traditional payment networks.

Regulation is another factor that will play a critical role in the future of cryptocurrencies as a practical currency. Currently, there is a lack of uniformity in how cryptocurrencies are regulated around the world, with some countries banning their use altogether. As more countries begin to regulate cryptocurrencies, it may become easier for businesses and consumers to use them in everyday transactions.

Despite these challenges, there are efforts being made to make cryptocurrencies more practical for everyday use. Some companies are working to create stablecoins, which are cryptocurrencies that are backed by a stable asset, such as the US dollar. This could provide a more stable means of exchange for consumers.

Additionally, some cryptocurrencies are implementing improvements to their networks, such as faster transaction times and lower fees, in order to make them more scalable and user-friendly.

Overall, the future outlook for cryptocurrencies as a practical currency is still uncertain. While there are challenges that need to be addressed, there are also promising developments being made to improve the practicality of cryptocurrencies. As adoption and regulatory clarity increase, it is possible that cryptocurrencies will become a more viable means of exchange in the future.

Chapter 6: Complex Technology
Explanation of the complex technology behind cryptocurrencies

Cryptocurrencies are digital or virtual currencies that rely on a complex network of technology to facilitate secure transactions. The underlying technology behind cryptocurrencies, known as blockchain, is a decentralized digital ledger that records and verifies transactions using cryptography. Blockchain technology is a complex and sophisticated system that relies on advanced computer algorithms, network protocols, and cryptographic techniques to ensure the integrity and security of the network.

The concept of blockchain technology was first introduced in 2008 with the launch of Bitcoin, the first and most well-known cryptocurrency. The success of Bitcoin and other cryptocurrencies has led to the development of a wide range of digital assets, each with its own unique features and characteristics.

The core principle of blockchain technology is decentralization, which means that there is no central authority controlling the network. Instead, transactions are validated and processed by a network of nodes spread across the globe. These nodes work together to reach a consensus on the validity of transactions, and once consensus is reached, the transaction is added to the blockchain ledger. This decentralized model is what gives blockchain its security and transparency, as every transaction is recorded and verified by the network, and no single entity has control over the system.

However, the complexity of blockchain technology can make it difficult for the average person to understand, and this has been a major barrier to the widespread adoption of cryptocurrencies. The technical jargon and complex concepts can be daunting for those who are not familiar with the technology, and this has led to a lack of understanding and trust in the system.

To address this challenge, there have been efforts to simplify the technology and make it more accessible to the general public. Some of the strategies that have been employed include creating user-friendly wallets and interfaces, developing educational resources and tutorials, and building communities of developers and enthusiasts who can share knowledge and provide support.

Despite the complexity of blockchain technology, its potential for disrupting traditional financial systems and transforming industries is significant. The security and transparency of the system, combined with its ability to facilitate fast and secure transactions, have the potential to revolutionize the way we do business and exchange value. As the technology continues to evolve and mature, we can expect to see new applications and use cases for blockchain and cryptocurrencies that we have not yet imagined.

Barriers to adoption for the average person

The complexity of the technology behind cryptocurrencies is one of the major barriers to adoption for the average person. While some people are comfortable using new technologies, many find the process of buying, storing, and using cryptocurrencies to be confusing and overwhelming. Cryptocurrencies are often associated with a steep learning curve, as users must navigate complex security features, complicated interfaces, and unfamiliar terminology.

One of the primary challenges for the average person is understanding the technical jargon and concepts associated with cryptocurrencies. Terms like "blockchain," "public key cryptography," and "mining" can be intimidating and difficult to comprehend, even for those with a background in computer science. In addition, the process of acquiring and storing cryptocurrencies can be challenging, as it often involves using specialized software and hardware, such as cryptocurrency wallets and cold storage devices.

Another barrier to adoption is the perceived risk associated with cryptocurrencies. Cryptocurrencies are often associated with high levels of volatility and risk, which can make the average person hesitant to invest in them. In addition, there have been numerous instances of fraud, theft, and hacking in the cryptocurrency space, which has eroded trust in the technology and made some people hesitant to use it.

Finally, the lack of user-friendly interfaces and intuitive design is a significant barrier to adoption for the average person. While there are some user-friendly platforms and wallets available, many cryptocurrency services are difficult to use and navigate. This can make the process of buying and using cryptocurrencies more time-consuming and frustrating than it needs to be.

Overall, the complex technology behind cryptocurrencies presents a significant barrier to adoption for the average person. However, there are steps that can be taken to make the technology more accessible and user-friendly, including the development of more intuitive interfaces and the creation of educational resources to help people understand the technology.

Opportunities and challenges for the future of cryptocurrency technology

As the technology behind cryptocurrencies continues to evolve, there are both opportunities and challenges that arise. Some of the opportunities include:

Greater efficiency: As the technology improves, the speed and efficiency of cryptocurrency transactions are likely to increase. This could make cryptocurrency a more viable alternative to traditional payment methods.

Improved security: One of the key benefits of cryptocurrency is the high level of security it provides. As the technology improves, this security is likely to become even stronger, making it more appealing to businesses and consumers.

Greater innovation: The decentralized nature of cryptocurrencies allows for greater innovation and experimentation. As new technologies emerge, they can be integrated into the cryptocurrency ecosystem, potentially creating new use cases and applications.

Financial inclusion: Cryptocurrency has the potential to improve financial inclusion by providing access to financial services for individuals who may not have access to traditional banking systems.

However, there are also several challenges that must be addressed in order for cryptocurrency technology to reach its full potential:

Scalability: As more people begin to use cryptocurrency, the existing technology may struggle to handle the increased demand. This could result in slower transaction times and higher fees.

Regulation: Cryptocurrencies exist in a regulatory gray area, with many governments struggling to determine how to classify and regulate them. This lack of clarity can create uncertainty for businesses and consumers.

Energy consumption: As discussed in the previous chapter, cryptocurrency mining requires significant energy consumption, which has environmental impacts. As the technology evolves, finding ways to reduce this energy consumption will be crucial.

User experience: Cryptocurrency can be challenging for the average person to use and understand, which creates a barrier to adoption. Improving the user experience and making cryptocurrency more accessible could help to overcome this challenge.

Overall, the future of cryptocurrency technology is full of promise, but there are also significant challenges that must be addressed. By focusing on these challenges and working to improve the technology, cryptocurrency has the potential to revolutionize the way we think about and use money.

Potential for simplification and mass adoption

As discussed earlier, the complex technology behind cryptocurrencies is one of the main barriers to their adoption. However, efforts are being made to simplify the technology and make it more accessible to the average person. One example of this is the development of user-friendly wallets and exchanges that make it easy to buy, sell, and store cryptocurrencies.

In addition, there are initiatives to make the underlying blockchain technology more user-friendly and accessible. For example, some blockchain projects are developing smart contracts that can be created and executed by non-programmers, which has the potential to greatly expand the use cases for blockchain technology.

Another opportunity for simplification and mass adoption is the development of stablecoins, which are cryptocurrencies that are pegged to the value of a stable asset like the U.S. dollar. These stablecoins offer a way to avoid the volatility that is often associated with traditional cryptocurrencies, which could make them more appealing to the average person.

However, there are still challenges to be overcome in order to achieve mass adoption. One major challenge is the scalability of blockchain technology. Currently, most blockchain networks have limited capacity, which can result in slow transaction times and high fees. This makes it difficult for cryptocurrencies to be used for everyday transactions like buying a cup of coffee. Efforts are being made to address this issue, such as the development of layer-two solutions like the Lightning Network, which allow for faster and cheaper transactions.

Another challenge is the lack of regulatory clarity around cryptocurrencies. Many countries have yet to establish clear regulations around the use of cryptocurrencies, which can create uncertainty and hinder adoption. However, some countries are taking steps to provide clarity, such as the recent passage of a comprehensive cryptocurrency bill in El Salvador.

Overall, there is great potential for simplification and mass adoption of cryptocurrency technology, but there are still challenges to be overcome. As the technology continues to evolve and improve, it is likely that we will see more widespread adoption of cryptocurrencies in the future.

Summary and Conclusion
Recap of the six bad things associated with cryptocurrencies

In this section, we will provide a recap of the six bad things associated with cryptocurrencies discussed in the previous chapters. We will also briefly discuss their impact and implications for the future of cryptocurrency.

The first bad thing associated with cryptocurrencies is their potential use in illegal activities, such as money laundering and tax evasion. While it is true that traditional currencies can also be used for such purposes, the anonymity and decentralization of cryptocurrencies make them more attractive to criminals.

The second bad thing is the high volatility and risk associated with cryptocurrency investments. This can lead to significant financial losses for investors who do not fully understand the market and the risks involved.

The third bad thing is the significant energy consumption and environmental impact of cryptocurrency mining, which can contribute to climate change and environmental degradation.

The fourth bad thing is the limited acceptance of cryptocurrencies in mainstream society, which can hinder their potential as a practical currency.

The fifth bad thing is the complex technology behind cryptocurrencies, which can be a barrier to adoption for the average person.

The sixth and final bad thing is the potential for cryptocurrency scams and fraud, which can result in significant financial losses for individuals and undermine trust in the entire cryptocurrency market.

While these bad things may seem daunting, it is important to note that many of them can be addressed through continued innovation, education, and collaboration within the cryptocurrency community.

For example, efforts to reduce the environmental impact of cryptocurrency mining are already underway through the development of more energy-efficient mining technology and the use of renewable energy sources.

Additionally, increased education and awareness about cryptocurrency scams and fraud can help individuals make more informed investment decisions and avoid falling victim to fraudulent schemes.

Furthermore, ongoing efforts to simplify the technology behind cryptocurrencies and increase their acceptance in mainstream society can help to make them more accessible and practical for everyday use.

Overall, while there are certainly challenges and risks associated with cryptocurrencies, there is also significant potential for their continued growth and development. By addressing the bad things associated with cryptocurrencies and working towards solutions, we can help to build a more sustainable and inclusive future for this emerging technology.

Reflection on the overall impact of cryptocurrencies on society

Over the past decade, cryptocurrencies have emerged as a new and rapidly growing industry that has the potential to transform the way people interact with money and financial systems. Despite the promise of decentralization and the potential for increased financial freedom, cryptocurrencies have also been associated with several negative impacts on society.

One of the most significant impacts of cryptocurrencies has been their role in facilitating illicit activities, such as money laundering and illegal transactions on the dark web. Additionally, the high energy consumption and carbon footprint associated with cryptocurrency mining has raised concerns about their negative impact on the environment. The lack of acceptance by mainstream society, complex technology, and high volatility also limit the practicality of cryptocurrencies as a mainstream form of currency.

Despite these challenges, the potential benefits of cryptocurrencies should not be overlooked. Cryptocurrencies have the potential to increase financial inclusion, provide greater access to financial services for underserved populations, and offer a new level of transparency in financial transactions. The decentralized nature of cryptocurrencies also has the potential to promote financial autonomy and reduce the influence of centralized financial institutions.

As the cryptocurrency industry continues to evolve, it is important for stakeholders to work together to address the negative impacts of cryptocurrencies and develop practical solutions that can unlock their full potential. This may include regulatory efforts to mitigate risks, increased investment in renewable energy to reduce the environmental impact of mining, and continued innovation to simplify the technology and increase accessibility for the average person.

In conclusion, while cryptocurrencies have several negative impacts on society, they also offer significant opportunities for positive change. It is up to society to determine the future of cryptocurrencies and work to realize their potential as a force for good in the financial world.

Call to action for investors, businesses, and policymakers

The call to action for investors, businesses, and policymakers is a critical aspect of any discussion on the impact of cryptocurrencies on society. With the increasing popularity of cryptocurrencies and their potential to disrupt traditional financial systems, it is essential that key players take steps to ensure that the benefits of this new technology are maximized while minimizing the risks.

Investors, for example, should be mindful of the potential risks associated with investing in cryptocurrencies and take appropriate steps to protect their investments. This may involve conducting due diligence on projects before investing, diversifying their portfolios, and monitoring market trends.

Businesses, on the other hand, should take a proactive approach to understanding cryptocurrencies and their potential impact on their industries. This may involve conducting research and development to identify opportunities to incorporate blockchain technology into their operations or exploring new business models that leverage the advantages of cryptocurrencies.

Policymakers also have a crucial role to play in shaping the regulatory environment around cryptocurrencies. As cryptocurrencies continue to gain in popularity, policymakers must work to strike a balance between protecting consumers and investors from potential fraud and abuse while also fostering innovation and competition in the market.

To that end, policymakers may consider implementing clear and consistent regulations that provide certainty and transparency for businesses and investors. They may also consider supporting research and development initiatives that explore the potential of cryptocurrencies and blockchain technology to address some of the most pressing challenges facing society, such as financial inclusion, supply chain transparency, and data privacy.

In summary, the call to action for investors, businesses, and policymakers is to take a proactive approach to understanding cryptocurrencies and their potential impact on society. By doing so, we can harness the benefits of this new technology while mitigating its risks and contributing to a more equitable and sustainable future for all.

Final thoughts on the future of cryptocurrencies

In recent years, cryptocurrencies have gained increasing attention and adoption in the financial industry, but their future is still uncertain. The potential benefits of cryptocurrencies, such as decentralized control and secure transactions, have been widely discussed, but there are also many challenges and risks associated with them. As we have explored in this report, there are six major bad things associated with cryptocurrencies: volatility, security, regulation, environmental impact, lack of acceptance, and complex technology.

Despite these challenges, there are opportunities for cryptocurrencies to evolve and become more widely accepted in the future. One such opportunity is the potential for increased innovation in the technology underlying cryptocurrencies, such as blockchain and distributed ledger technology. This innovation could lead to improvements in security and speed of transactions, as well as the potential for increased interoperability between different cryptocurrencies.

In addition, efforts to increase education and awareness around cryptocurrencies could also contribute to their wider adoption. By providing more information and resources to investors, businesses, and policymakers, the potential benefits of cryptocurrencies can be better understood and balanced against the risks.

It is important for investors, businesses, and policymakers to take a proactive approach to addressing the challenges and risks associated with cryptocurrencies. This includes efforts to improve the security of transactions, reduce the environmental impact, increase acceptance, and simplify the technology for the average person. Additionally, policymakers may need to consider new regulations to ensure the safe and ethical use of cryptocurrencies.

In conclusion, the future of cryptocurrencies is uncertain, but there is potential for continued growth and development in the industry. It is important for all stakeholders to approach cryptocurrencies with a balanced perspective, acknowledging both the potential benefits and risks, and taking proactive steps to address the challenges and ensure a sustainable and responsible future for cryptocurrencies.

THE END

Potential References

Chapter 1: Introduction to Cryptocurrencies

Nakamoto, S. (2008). Bitcoin: A Peer-to-Peer Electronic Cash System. https://bitcoin.org/bitcoin.pdf

Tapscott, D., & Tapscott, A. (2016). Blockchain revolution: how the technology behind bitcoin is changing money, business, and the world. Penguin.

Chapter 2: Cryptocurrency Investment and Trading

Popper, N. (2014). Digital Gold: Bitcoin and the Inside Story of the Misfits and Millionaires Trying to Reinvent Money. Harper Collins.

Antonopoulos, A. M. (2014). Mastering Bitcoin: Unlocking Digital Cryptocurrencies. O'Reilly Media.

Chapter 3: Blockchain Technology and Its Applications

Swan, M. (2015). Blockchain: Blueprint for a new economy. O'Reilly Media.

Don Tapscott (2018). Blockchain Revolution: How the Technology Behind Bitcoin and Other Cryptocurrencies Is Changing the World. Penguin Random House.

Chapter 4: Cryptocurrency Security and Privacy

Bonneau, J. (2015). Bitcoin and Cryptocurrency Technologies: A Comprehensive Introduction. Princeton University Press.

Mougayar, W. (2016). The Business Blockchain: Promise, Practice, and Application of the Next Internet Technology. Wiley.

Chapter 5: Cryptocurrency Regulations and Risks

Rusu, L., & Marcut, M. (2018). Cryptocurrency: Challenges and Opportunities for Financial Crime, Money Laundering, and Tax Evasion. Procedia Economics and Finance, 46, 473-478.

European Central Bank. (2019). Crypto-Assets: Implications for financial stability, monetary policy, and payments and market infrastructures. ECB Occasional Paper Series, (223), 1-43.

Chapter 6: Cryptocurrencies and Society

Vigna, P., & Casey, M. J. (2015). The Age of Cryptocurrency: How Bitcoin and Digital Money are Challenging the Global Economic Order. St. Martin's Press.

Narayanan, A., Bonneau, J., Felten, E., Miller, A., & Goldfeder, S. (2016). Bitcoin and Cryptocurrency Technologies: A Comprehensive Introduction. Princeton University Press.Summary and Conclusion

Coindesk. (2021). Bitcoin Price Index. https://www.coindesk.com/price/bitcoin

CoinMarketCap. (2021). Cryptocurrency Market Capitalizations. https://coinmarketcap.com/

www.ingramcontent.com/pod-product-compliance
Lightning Source LLC
LaVergne TN
LVHW010409070526
838199LV00065B/5921